Of modern lowercase jottings

It is the effect of modern lowercase jottings,
That spew out dust as dry as deserts,
To enter the eyes and sop up all liquid fantasy,
Until my brain swims none and dries like skull.
Those cold and simple, clean little whimpers,
Posting absurdities, absolving conclusions never,
Unfounded, baseless, efficient like skyscrapers,
Desperate for feeling, clinging to the left margin,
Needing punctuation, refusing personality,
Expressing spirit only as spirit wanting expression.

My words, like artifacts of some grand emotion,
That lived long ago and surely did exist
Will announce that true poetry was not at rest,
Though I cannot, in archaic manner, use dead words:
Thus my modern lines are handicapped.
Bend down and peer in to my glassy vision,
My eyes! like windows to a wonder-filled land
Shall tell of inconstant realities, and not the real world,
Where dreams of brave hope may live nurtured
And sleep well in the blissful bed of the mind,

And I, like a flower in a barren nation,
Shewing petals to fall and fly where they may,
While my heart beats loudly—rivers of blood!
With difficulty I ground and do not float away,
These currents! These waters that flow
Through my soul, I pour them forth uneasily,
Like a channeler transmitting codes from afar,
I open my pen and blurt for recorded mankind
The songs of my heart, the wild sensations:
A task done in pain but not in vain.

Oh You Pretty Flower

Oh you pretty flower,
What mold were you made from?
Tell me where and in what direction
So I may start my run.
I'll offer it my protection,
It will suffer no imperfection!

If I could capture your beauty
Into the seed of a plant,
I'd plant a thousand of you
And make a wondrous view,

And with the great sun's duty
A field of you I'd grow,
Each day I'd see your beauty
From these seeds that I did sow,

Who dares to pluck you from
The place that you do know?
He gathers a bouquet of you little flowers
As if you alone were not enough,
It is he that grasps your tender limbs
With hands that are so rough,

He collects beauty like money
As if it could be manufactured,
Oh he does not see your elegance,
He only speaks of your irrelevance,

That mold I did speak of before—
Its existence is forever no more,
He does not see you are unique,
He does not reap your grand mystique,

Oh you pretty little flower,
Tell me this is true:
That man you'd rather be with
Is me, this man with you.

I conduct the subliminal chorus

I conduct the subliminal chorus...
Birds, fly from tree! Wind, lift them up!
Sun, warm the backs of creatures, the tops of trees
    and the heads of men!
I, walk along. You, keep by my side.
Earth, stand firm! Sky, dome us all.
Soporific night, delay your darkness!
Gravity, loosen your grip!
Clouds, prepare for my coming! My body will
    join where my mind already lives.
Peace, enter me! Love, swim in my blood.
Sweet air, sugarcoat my lungs!
Recondite knowledge, fill my brain to the brim!
Life, help me to never need Regret.

Nature simply whispered to me

Nature simply whispered to me
All her secrets of glaring glee,
I let her in to fill my eyes
And my stare went not unnoticed,

She saw in me propriety
And chiefly wanted to know
Why I felt it so
That I should mingle with society,

I simply cried at this
As one absent from bliss,
Still basking in that beauty
I thought of relinquishing all duty.

To Alicia, In a Land of Unicorns

Alicia, in dying young, I want for you
Some remembrance of your living honor,
For you who dared to love this soul
And raise it to your state of high enchantment,

For you, my noble friend, I bleed forth
An ocean of dutiful respect and honor,
In striving to pay some rent
For our lovely times, our coupled passions,

For you I weep, who loved to dream of castles,
Who in each day tried earnestly to hold on
To swirls of color and fantastic feelings
Felt in a blissful night's dream,

With me you danced with butterflies
And though at times we lay to cry our sorrows
We bravely thought the world to be
Under celestial magic—a place for fairies,

And we left responsibility, somewhere behind,
To lay by the sea under the midday sun,
To wet our bodies in the tumbling waves,
To read books that promised forever on another side,

And often I would join you and end myself
For residence in that land of unicorns,
It is for you I live and contemplate magic
Though my inspiration be far removed from me,

Oh untimely death! Unfinished life!
What robbery to me and all the land!
If only your tired soul, sickened with strife,
Had firmly grasped my outstretched hand!

No written word may give consolation,
What earnest language could be so deep
As to reach you now, while in coffin you sleep,
Or soothe your soul where it may be?

But I develop my soul so you may see
And so I may in time be with you,
In blissful stride on this cosmic ride
Or in a land of unicorns, roaming free!

What yonder music rings?

What yonder music rings?
It is that bell that tolls the morning:
The chirping of birds happier than I,
Triumphant sky illuminates once more
Like an eternal awakening,
Away with darkness and clear from heavy fog,
And the sun bravely rises,
What courage is the new day!
And what marvels exist about me!
What stirs within me that is not good?
How can a poet calmly look on
Without wonder and merriment?
Earth can be no more beautiful than she is now,
It could never be a braver picture than this!
And now I dress as if in costume to a ball
And desire openness with no walls
But walls I impose around me,
The earth is open and I am open!
Everything is good and mesmerizing!
Everything is as I'd have it to be,
All is what I desire,
And no thing can escape this love!
My heart is awakened, my eyes open fully,
No blindness for this is clear to me:
I am everything and everything is me,
Just as I would have it to be!

Forgive me if I hum loudly

Forgive me if I hum loudly today,
For you see, I have been lifted from a deep despair
Since this morning, and if only for a short time
I may sense some jovial truths in the air
'Til the end of this day's chime,
Then I will fall back under the press
Of some divine mysterious darkness,
So forgive me if I hum loudly today,

And please grant your pardon
If I whistle a tune loudly to the sky,
Scarcely before has my soul sung a song,
For Hope today is calling from on high,
And how could heaven call to me?
Just walking here so gallantly with eyes fixed on the ground,
My head rose up as if to answer a sound
And Hope was there, all around, pulsing from the sky!

Dear Philosopher

If human bodies rendered not our time as bound,
If copious pleasures unfolded through each day,
Then it would be right and also merry
That you should sit a while and stay,

For the man that thinks of reason,
Of vacuous spaces, infinite distances of mind,
Should ever have allowances many
To endlessly converse with his kind,

But dear philosopher, tell me:
With winter-cracked hands that pound away,
Or silent farmers with bent backs—
How shall they enter mental play?

As you sat and pondered unknown books,
The laborer has come with scratching plow
With which he feeds your growing belly,
Yet you find him dank and smelly,

If all harbored books and purses robust:
More songs from those hearts, books from those hands,
Not silently dumb and locked to their lands
But loudly faithful in brotherly trust!

I notice the sun

I notice the sun as it settles in the west:
A pool of fire sizzling in the piney horizon,
And my mind does wail, "Come back, oh sun!"
For I've sepulchered my talents behind house doors
Entranced by matters of trivial meaning,
And what was missed? A grand promised bliss!
Dear Sun! On knees I beg for your stay!
Oh give me another chance at this day,
Sun, as you hurriedly flee from the night,
My lesson is learned, it serves me right,
For each lovely day is but a turn,
No longer for more time will I yearn,
And forever this hallowed day is lost!
Tonight I shall tally at what cost.

I dare not stomp an ant

I dare not stomp an ant,
I barely know that I am I,
And all the world could go to war,
I would be left wanting more.

Seems there is no other, for we are one,
And compassion is my chosen gun.
When Love has won the game
We all feel the same.

I would if I could

I would if I could, fly away,
Go wherever on earth I may,
Leave prison by morn
And have a day well worn.

I said "If I could fly"
I might not want to die,
If weight was not on top of me
Some wind might come to carry me.

If I had Hope and Concentrate
My mental powers flourish,
But my focus doesn't abdicate,
I simply want to fly.

Something free inside of me
Craves its time to come
But until wings sprout from back
There's no adventure—none.

Heaven's Gate

Heaven's gate is a mental block
Bolted in ground for souls that fly,
And just as prominent as the ticking clock
Which limits and with illusion steals,

Fasten that lock and unroll the scroll,
I never doubted the greatness of my soul.
But tell your friend where his soul began
And he'll doubt you with the anger of man.

Education makes erect

Education makes erect
The plowman and the farmer
For even fools use farming tools
And his book is such a charmer.

The antiquity of the book
Far precedes some earth
And the principles all around
Are even better than tilling ground.

I crave a world to call my own

I crave a world to call my own,
And in my silly way may roam
Into the walled forests free,
There let no beast harass me.

And play all day in the strand,
Or sleeping quiet on the sand,
Alone, there let nobody be,
There let no eye watch over me.

I crave a house to call my home,
In silence read insightful tome,
When life's no more in front of me
There let me sleep eternally.

Plan B

I think I'd like a book
To read outdoors in spring
And for every gentle morning
To hear the small birds sing.

I'd like to take some simple food—
Roasted meats and jam,
And live as though the Amish do:
A babe in Nature's pram.

If I had my own plantation
This is what I'd see:
Endless flowers with rows of beans
And I'd call it Innisfree.

I want to feel the seasons,
To sense I am alive,
To live deliberately—
Just the sun and me.

When hearing grand orchestral music

When hearing grand orchestral music,
I do curiously contemplate if ever
My dutiful permutations extensive
Shall explode as stormy weather,
Or soothe and coat, then fire
The brain like a furnace insane,
To keep the spirits afloat
From a literary symphony I wrote.
And my music that sounds in the head
Equaling a gathering tempest fed,
Supplied with wings that soar with birds
For I shall write a symphony of words!

Eden

They said I could have Eden
If only I'd believe,
Put my faith in hopeful thoughts
And Eden I'll receive.

I think I could have flowers
Planted everywhere,
And peace in every moment
Just hanging in the air.

Is bliss in future times
Or happening in the now?
With temp of present climes
It's difficult to dowse.

Upon being scolded for not talking

To socialize is death,
People charge a fee—
Must interact to exist
In loud society,

Quiet is the key
And chatter I impeach,
They truly do not know,
They use their vocal speech,

Solitude is sound to me,
Relationships are doomed,
Who has not loved his silence
Has truly not yet bloomed.

She

She hears no evil,
She barely sees sin,
She rests upon a sylvan den.

When father dies at close of day
The moon, the moon, the moon,
Rises and not too soon.

A certain part, fancy and free
Develops deep within me
And they call her Liberty.

I AM

I am sexless and immortal,
I am Being, I am Man.
Don't call me crazy
Just like Pan.

I am the measure, I am man,
I am the circle eternal,
I am heavenly infernal
Lamp of Ages.

I am ineffable essence,
The colored substance,
Yes Infinity, the finite me,
Dared frame the symmetry.

Adonis Aubade

I could weep for this Adonis,
The source of all my warmth,
He is missing every day
And there is but one way
For him to sail in,

I must sacrifice the selfish heart,
Drive the chariot of my load
And royally perform my part—
Then He will rise on the horizon
In a sailing ship by dawn.

Papa Legba

Papa Legba, hold me tonight,
Tell me a story, make things right,
Give me a message from far beyond,
Papa your word is your bond,

I pray you play no tricks,
To please open the gate
For my soul is surely lost
And you know my fate,

I have learned of your games
But you hold the key,
Good God set me free,
Make way for opportunity.

A lizard in the sun

Like a lizard in the sun
Which does survey and run
The entire sum of his kingdom
On his imperial throne
Which is a blazing stone,

I will conquer my own earth,
Yes the breadth and the girth,
Put down my own revolt,
I will win at my own life
Whatever Success asks of price.

Who does want another life?
In the stillness is a force
Endlessly beckoning me to the Source:
"Conquer the material plane
For then you will be sane."

How Sumptuous, To Read the Books

How sumptuous, to read the books,
To know some secrets, at last!
And take a myriad of looks
At a quiet recondite blast,

The simple idea, hidden for long,
Perhaps in parameter of a song
And taken down, by me, a simple note
That others present block and smote,

And ignorance is a hateful thing,
For books are dams unto a spring,
Then study all, like unto another,
And boisterous findings there unsmother.

Awe is separate longing

Awe is separate longing
For a cloud, a wave, a hill,
Apart from what we long to be,
An old family memory:
The stars are my pedigree.
The clouds, my progeny.

Father

Father, tell me the meaning of 311,
Teach me to count to twenty-three,
Unfold the documents before my eyes,
The plans, mysterious and dumb to me.

Show me how to sow the clouds
Upon the glowing earth,
And how to conquer all
The seekers of this mirth.

Father, spell out progeny
On a tablet, paper or clay,
And usher in a Union,
For even peasants may,

When given the pure prescription,
Become unafraid, unlost.
This is the herd's condition:
Cold lambs in the forest,

Even the herd on the hill,
In perfect loving trust,
Is looking for you, Father,
Why don't you visit us?

Symbolic Shepherd upon a cloud,
Or hiding in the dark,
Explain to us and act as proud
Or show the artist's mark.

If I were bound to Nature

If I were bound to Nature
Like a shepherd,
And could count from the twinkling sky
Some astrology or appropriation to Life,

Then as the ancient stargazer
Under a mystical ceiling I'd breathe,
Not contained
But ever swimming in the above.

Bleaching Grounds of Guideway

I was arrested by a cloud
Made immense and bold up there,
And I am not too proud
To say I breathed with silent care,

I know that they will speak of me
As they did with Emily:
"A rich inner life"
Because a cloud has soothed my strife,

I'd be the cloud if I knew
I am immortal sky,
I'd even skim the treetops
If I didn't have to try,

Desire is labor to the soul
If it remains unaware
That the clouds have him
And he has all that is there.

Often there's a tired plane

Often there's a tired plane
Yearning over the fields,
A single-engine fellow,
I wonder how he feels,

I listen closely
To judge his path,
He has his freedom
And views so vast!

Lonely through the silent air
He soars as birds may,
And though I am no pilot
I feel that I shall fly one day.

If through the atmosphere came a teacher

If through the atmosphere came a teacher
From the skies descending to the dusty ground,
To tell the reasons for the seasons changing
Or of the reverberating frequencies around,
Then the humble ones are freshly enlightened.
The newcomer is held as the busy god,
Revelations fell from above—a beneficent entrustment!
Though I infer those secrets of success,
Making me seem as one equally blessed,
What is preferred is the alien wisdom sent down,
Not the ancient pagan equilibrium of earth.
To the fault of priestly men in town
The new religion scrambled into an evil birth,
Thus all posterity in heavenly trance.

My job is student

My job is student—
Not plowman or farmer,
And never before has such an occupation
Been mixed with recreation,

I'd tell my dead fathers
Of universities,
But never would they laugh more
And mock my books in heavy store,

Because I know not labor,
I know not Chance,
And never could I cultivate the plant,
But I call the Truth an aspiration.

Wild Horses

This love is wild horses,
I barely eat and gasp my breaths
Before Recompense gallops again
And sleep becomes sweet, sleep becomes sweet.

There is adventure now
And I'm lost somehow,
Time is shamed and my gain
Is eternal cool, eternal cool.

There is but one

There is but one of such import
To me that wealth seems mockery
Of the blissed union we report
And for my lonely idol there is missing
To sing your praises, a chorus,
Let other things bore us!
For even fame is but shame
Contrasted to pleasing my master
And if they say this love is sin
Then in that realm they won't get in,
Where Love's heart pulses the center of all
They can't come in, no not at all.

If I feared not fun to be made

If I feared not fun to be made
Of you and I, or you alone,
One secret confession 'til then delayed,
Before I'm laid in ground and marked with stone,
Would be placed by my bed—I would admit
That with silent admirations and hidden gaze
I counted your beauty but could not commit
This knowledge, not even among friends,
Lest they suggest me a sufferer of dreams
Or far begone from my unworthy home.
And though such as I have quiet affairs,
If with you I'd announce in indignant tone,
Forget opinions, and become blind to stares,
So that I might not love alone.

To my love unarrived

Such wondrous places shall we nuzzle:
May park or July forest,
Many moments left in puzzle,
Counting less our daily money,
Rather eat our morning honey
And ripe fruits in blazing climes—
May Gratitude pay for times
Well spent in vibrant love
Under fairy skies above.

Today the apples are plump and firm

Today the apples are plump and firm
On all your cheeks, milky-white flesh
And red blush rightly do affirm
And attest, your youth is fresh.
But few jolts, marks from living,
What all count as recreation and fun
Shall bruise and test the rest
And all enjoy cookery of the sun
While tender fruit is by life consumed;
It is best now to be bitten,
To hasten towards love, stash away books,
Enjoy Youth's reign while Fortune looks;
Night follows day, enjoy your power
For this is the time, now is the hour.

I love you mostly for your deeds

I love you mostly for your deeds
Which advance beyond my novice gratitude.
My soul learns lessons it chiefly needs
To act in your way with wondrous attitude.
Not just for your body with sculpted contour,
Although I might easily write its praises
With a poet's trumped-up phrases—
You extract and draw much loftier plans
Exampling what those do not know,
For your hands are the world's hands,
Because it may blossom and grow
But cannot say, "Here, please enjoy."
Thus your heart beats with the world's heart
And you the exemplar of Nature's beauty.

I leave thoughts of you with every step

I leave thoughts of you with every step,
Every footstep leaves a faint impression
Of you, where you have touched the earth
Through my mind with every remembrance
That sits in this head and is brewed
By the blazing sun and rises from me in wispy fumes,
Distilling the air around with love,
In so that each who steps there or sits this spot
Shall feel a tiny jolt and sense a certain air
Of peace and love, as if the Universe strikes
This place I've been a shrine to you.

To all the flowers

To all the flowers I have picked
I must apologize.
How brave you were to boldly grow
Beneath the hot blue skies.

No one warned your sudden death
Or knew your life's content,
That flowering is the plant's aspiration,
Yet all remain ignorant of effort spent.

To grow, to renew, to become the highest
Is the flower upon earth
Showing all who are the shyest
How to burst into rebirth.

My Mind Can

My mind can and my body can do,
In infinite potential, it's so very true
That my mouth does speak, may the Universe obey
All my heart and mind does say.

If I hold a picture in palm of my hand
It dissolves and blows like a weathering sand
Into the ether, beyond the Me,
And forms an object most effortlessly.

Forever in action, like a vibrating dream,
Endlessly flowing—a full-throated stream:
No thing at all is as it may seem.

When I consider this love

When I consider this love from objective view,
If as from overhead I examine us two:
All senses lost, emotions reign illogical
As slaves to mental desires, incarnate
As impoverished hearts with thirsty beats,
Animalistic as pheromones of the body's breath.
When the chemicals do churn and slush,
As blocking my mind, an inward hush
Consumes us both in dumb ecstasy.
The youth-strained elders condemn our acts,
But if upon a table I examine the facts:
No fool's heart is mine; In perfect sense
Us two as parts of an equation divine,
I feel it now, for no fool's heart is mine!

Of things to come

If, all at once, you could see
The bursting of all the flowers,
The future events in unison,
And judge the world with all its powers,

If, in a hurry, you could hear
Your destiny's unfolding,
(A bleeding thunder to your ear)
And not participate the ever-molding,

If all the sunsets flashed your eye
Then you would not on your pillow cry
But inhale fear and exhale air
For the world is ever changing.

The Mind Can Heal

Dis-ease is brought by mind,
Invited from within—
Not resting in body unwelcome,
Go to the hospital and tell them!

The currents blocked
Will scream their arrest—
Of obstruction built by stress,
And mind can heal, as body can.

Some thirsts just need water

Some thirsts just need water,
Not bubbly soda drinks,
Or jeweled star upon the hand
That ushers plenty thanks,

But if true drought upon the soul
You easily could see,
No haughty compliment blankly told
And no thoughtless gifts for me.

Lakshmi, grant my boons

Lakshmi, grant my boons,
Exponent my wealth, outside
As well as in spirit deep.
Ganesha please do sweep
Away the obstacles!
And Eros, as for love, show me some.
Gum Gum Gum Gum

No Borders

There are no borders,
You do as you like,
And love is the law
So love with might.

My name is Thelma,
I'm best of my region,
Love only me
Because hate is treason.

Experience

After seeking knowledge you shall find
The secret was within your mind
And after soaking knowledge up,
Drink no more, you are the cup,

Turn to the sky and feel that man
Create the world with your own hand,
Then wonder alone will suffice
And then you will have been born twice.

Love is the sun

Love is the sun raining forth
Without judgment and without birth
Like a secret conspiring cohort
And I believe I am a port.

So let me a vessel be
Simply sitting under a tree,
Writing and scrying a simple song,
And surely it will not be long

'Til man and god can be as one
For under the sun it is already done.

I felt such oneness

I felt such oneness with other folks
I mistook myself as the sole heir,
That I could arrive at home
And find no one waiting there,

But time proved the others
Returned to their skins,
Could I draw them to oneness
With the sponge of love?

The absorption happened quick
Though the rapture was temporal,
In each soul I saw evolution which
Is the journey of the world.

I began to worship all,
The wealthy and the poor,
I began to connect eyes
And found all wanting more,

Oh fragile sleeping people:
Feel the Breath, awake anew!
Our mother waits for us
Like the sun upon the dew.

Liberty

The time is now,
Let us go to the open field,
Let us build a fire
To illuminate the night.
She is a pale reflection
Of her golden father,
She is full of might tonight.

Let us play the flute, drink of grapes,
Be ancient for a while,
That curious deer may witness
I have the animal's secret,
Where are my clothes?
Where is the clothing of the world?

Where is the book
On water into wine?
I could dance away from right,
There is freedom in the night,
If I harm none what have I done?

I am remembering the journey
But forgetting the day,
My friend, were you in pain?

Where has the real me gone?
I am the earth, I am that tree,
We are living ecstasy.

Ego in the drawer

The silence of this cricket night
Has even convinced me more
That a sound must be made
And put my ego in the drawer.

Because, Because the Universe
May ask a price—
Not for me the flashing lights,
Not for me a lusty vice.

I might command a thousand wonders
By universal invitation at the door—
To be of service and print some poems
I put my ego in the drawer.

That man

That man, he did not answer me
But Nature won't go silently,
Yet everywhere and all around
There were no words, no sound.

Nature still she tortures me
With her never-ending glaring glee,
I believe the birds fly happily
And never a day did work.

The creatures of the woods
Enjoy everlasting gardens,
Yet never with a fork did pitch
Nor plant a seed from town,

How often I have eaten free
A potato from my bin,
Neither did I toil or spin,
She says ingratitude is sin.

Indifference

The world is so indifferent,
Yet I am not unkind
As to publish thoughts of hate
Or loose them from my mind.

The winds are unforgiving,
The ground welcomes my tears,
Please deliver me to Home
From blind and deaf peers.

Forces of Hate

The forces of Hate tear us apart
Thinking ego is pure of heart
And claiming portrait of God's own face,
But space is such a quiet place.

Here on earth grows a love
Tolerant as spring to the flower,
A new emerging power
As certain as the dove.

Time rolls with patient skill
Through the angry forest of Hate,
My friends, you shall heal
And Love shall not abate.

There is nothing

There's nothing in this life,
I'd sweep away the years
But not that I hear you say
You'll wipe away the tears.

Every promised sugar moment
Was duller than the bread,
But for your radiant face
The papers report me dead.

HIM

Bake a cake for me and let it rot,
Then bring it to me in a pot,
Drizzle honey atop anew
And present it to me like a stew.

Give me honey cakes and dew
And all your worship too,
Mind the soul, salute the sun
But give me honey cakes and dew,
Yes all your worship too.

Resurrection

I'll dust off a brazen statue,
Give offerings of faith and hope,
I will sacrifice my doubt,
I'm too young to let my candle out,

I am the April Fool,
I have learned at my own school
And I've thoroughly searched the tomb:
All life escapes the womb.

Invocation

I call upon the higher spirits,
The inhabitants of invisible planes,
The keepers of secret knowledge
And protectors of mankind,

Only love-thoughts are here
And only the expansion of love.
Hear me! I conjure your assistance
In the Great Work of infinity,

We will be used, together conspiring,
I attract you! I attract you!
I call upon the invisible servants of goodness
To rain love down on me.

I will disperse, I will give
Of all abundance that springs forth,
I will be your earthly fount,
I am the channel,
Our wills are one.

Je suis illuminé

This life is everything you've asked for
Tempered by what you deserve,
This earth is heaven now,
The balance of karma is absurd.

Through every cause and effect
All desires will be met,
You will be led, you will be led,
And every debt will be fed.

I too am inebriate of air,
Je suis illuminé,
Everything deserves only awe,
Whatever comes to me.

Though I know it all
Mystery hangs like dew
'Til the final gasp that day
When I become you.

A Leaf That Fell

A leaf that fell
   Was directed to me
Because it hit my head
   As it fell from the tree,

As it brushed my hair
   With gentle purpose
I knew its meaning
   I knew its care,

It wanted me to know
   That it was there
To stop and look
   At its former abode

And to truly know
   That leaves may fall
At any time
   To answer my call,

That time sheds all
   And leaves must fall,
Then leaves become
   What they started from.

I was suddenly displeased

I was suddenly displeased with the sounds of the world,
The endless ruckus, the always chattering.
A schism happened in my brain, my eyes closed in disgust,
And I craved silence for the first time,

To be like the crab on a distant shore so quiet,
Digging warm sand into a burrow of solitude,
With nothing else but the wave's tumbling roar
And the seagull's overhead call.

Even the great lion on a savanna so endless
Hears only his guttural roar, and yes too
An overhead bird speaking of its freedom.

So I saw that I should be quiet for a while,
Indoors, confined, reading of the deep blue ocean
To mute all else and be with the world as I could.

To Jesse, Upon My Leaving

Hold it now—my memory,
And if ever hidden, search it out,
'Tis always near, no further than a contact,
No closer than I can travel,

Be it slow to flutter forth,
It will surely reach you again,
In surges outthought of,
In winds yet unborn your way,

On profound shores,
On transcendent mountains,
Under azure hue, same as ancient skies,
You may find my soul,

Taking notes on the beauty,
Studying scrolls of knowledge,
Whispering tales of friendship
To fly upon your breast,

As warm breezes, remembered smells,
Stirring up youthful broth,
Shaking membranes of every cell,
Filling you with a semblance of my being.

Slam not my name for leaving soon,
Have I not been called away?
Forget me often, remember me thus more,
And keep you head held high today,

Shallow souls do knock you down,
On dark paths by unpleasant entities,
Greatness our burden, love is our way,
We never among equals,

Hold it now, 'til tomorrow life,
When barely hidden, my kindred friend,
Different forms then, but divine souls find divine souls,
'Tis always near, search me out.

Ode to Orton Plantation

Often, while in urban shelter or glassy building,
    I regress to this place, this ideal spot
Where earth's riches, so heavily manicured, seem
    As showing Nature's true way of presenting herself,
And if I and all the world were left alone,
    In this way would we present ourselves,
Then all would be as this plantation.

This true Eden, if I shall ever see one,
    Full of mossy oaks that wave
Their gray hair over a rich garden blooming,
    As if to spread mystery in the air
Around every bush and over every flower,

Then fowl scatter down from space
    And swoop into the wet rice fields,
As I watch from a white belvedere,
    Under me are grasses, figured in shape
Like a butterfly, and I know not what holds me,
    My feet are weightless, My heart catches air
And I will soon soar with the birds
    In that refuge of solitude.

I could not swim in the lagoon,
    I could not disturb the turtle's watery abode,
I dare not splash his sacred waters,
    And there too the alligator silently sits,
In him the archaic dinosaur longs for glorious days,
    He waits for something, From a distance
I wait with him.

Shortly over, the white antebellum mansion
    Triumphantly stands with grandness of the Parthenon,
Nestled by two wings to brace the earth,
    Lest it float on high with the clouds
As a stately pleasure-dome decreed.

If I could inquire some lone gardener,
   He might speak a tale, like a sage,
Of two fairies who, in early sunrise,
   Pranced on the front lawn with tiny feet,
All wet with morning dew, as they smuggled crumbs
   From the house, but stopped to kiss a flower.

The red Indian, the Confederate captain,
   All fought their woes on this hallowed land
Among history's strife and misfortune's gloom,
   And in the small cemetery, among dead fathers,
Sits King Moore's tomb, the great proprietor,
   In the shade, with gray monuments,
I think of my own ancestors.

In me live the woes of all dead fathers,
   And the passions of all hearts through millennia,
In me too the inheritance of the world's grandeur,
   I dare not ask what black business fed this place,
But here, time stops, and I am given a short life
   To promulgate some goodness, as Nature does,
I carry not the past, I embrace the dawn…

Surely We Shall Ever Be

When all alone I count my friends
I count your face the most,
Being of such shape and form
That, full of smiled blessings, uniform
Remembrances fill my mind,
I stare not at the ground,
Upon you I gaze,

Even as clouds, in pairs, fly through sky
Then so it must be you and I
Forever entwined with an astral thread,
And like two souls with but one head
Our thoughts, entirely interfused and near
That you are with me, I with you, my dear,
So surely we shall ever be
Two locked souls in company.

I wish I could meet a poet

I wish I could meet a poet
And talk of merry man:
How one may write, another fight,
But all try as best they can,

And wander the valleys deep with sorrow,
Or climb the peaks to salute the sun,
Our blessed meeting not ending the morrow
For befriending a poet is such fun!

Our endless talks, our shared years
In understanding, compassionate tears
Would then flow like rain on the ocean
When two poets, together, in motion.

I know not where I left my poet friend,
In what past life we last did meet,
When we two did face the sad fiend,
Together, 'til our last greet.

For time, it runs a never-ending line,
And I know not where you'll be,
While the breath of the sun is mine
Your soul, like a fish, in an abysmal sea.

To the Smoker on the Bench

Do not hang your head so low
  As happy crowds pass you by,
Do not stare at the ground like that,
  But rather raise your head to the sky
To see what is happening there,
  Oh you, who is full of care,
Do not be this isolated island,
  Full of inner weight,
As grass and trees and people
  Everywhere grow in sunlight,
But we may not relate.

Sun and clouds and shine are fine,
  They do not light the inner parts of you,
Oh he who of inner mysterious thoughts does pine
  Has a soul soured more by such an imposing view!

Pantheistic Poem

The weight of the world was ever swirling,
Two-ton clouds infuriate the sky,
The weight of death was the full-bodied sea
While rambunctious creation rolled by.

The wind had a rhythm that I dared not aspire,
And the birds flew, though I stay on ground,
My thoughts carried curious tokens higher
When no mover started commotion all around.

A sense sublime that boils within
Gathers deep wonders, emergent truth,
Of a secret disguise so thin:
The initial suspicions of my youth.

That though I did not plant the tree,
I turn my back, and watch, you'll see,
The tree grows not when I don't watch:
The universe needs me.

The winds that run from me, the air,
They need my lungs to call them fair
And if I did not swim the sea
It would dry up without my glee.

Some probe and say it must be God.
I know not how we came to be,
But hesitate not and remember your worth,
For human mind holds universal girth.

In a place without time

In a place without time a figure in black
Crossed my heart and I won't turn back,
By a barn beside the road all I heard was a toad—
Then a laugh in the night which gave me a fright,

Stalks of corn which sparkled by moon
Let loose from their depths a cowering coon
And all around swimming through fog
Were night animals straight from the bog.

I subdued my fear and there came a man
Who laughed at me and extended his hand,
He played a guitar and plucked every string
But I brought out a pen, said "writing's my thing,"

He wrote on paper a power song
And beseeched that I present it to the throng
That they would listen to my every sob
After I give it to the maddening mob.

Beyond the Rainbow

I drifted upon a palace
And instantly could see
What man-made mountains,
What spires of stone,
What wealth and gold could be!

I travelled to a tower
And peeked on sundry sights
And languished in the stillness
As clouds with castles strolled by,
Up there on great heights.

What I craved most
Through all my flights
Is now such wealth to me—
Twas moments of divinity
When I taste what freedom could be.

Generation

I toppled an obelisk in to the sea
And watched what came back up at me:
First just sprays of briny foam
From Poseidon's water home.

I put a seed in to the ground
And waited for a great big sound:
First patience came, then fortitude
In my dirty solitude.

Helplessly, the seed, it grew
Whether or not it wanted to
And desperately burst with no implore
As if ground never grew before,

Then dolphins came right near the shore
And dancing there formed a disc
Swimming around an askew obelisk.
Seems everything is listening.

New York is Forbidden Fruit

New York is forbidden fruit,
The apple of my eye,
And Central Park is Shangri-la,
I've been so far gone from Home.

Home is where I cannot go,
I cannot taste that tree,
Tall towers sweet to me
But I cannot pay the fee.

Ode to the Sun

May the Sun's rise hear applause,
May every blade of grass feel an inward stirring
And stretch out their arms.

New energy sprays through the atmosphere
Affording all life and the two types of growth
And I will bow. I will bow.

Look! The glory of this morning is the dawning
Of our foretold New Age—Only the dawning
But we can wait some more.

The cool night is over and the tramplings
Of life will begin. Thankless job!:
Infinite supply of energy and love.

Awaken me to a new day refreshed
And make erect all that are limp and asleep.
May all the earthly creatures understand
The humble worship of a star.

Purpose

I know I've asked for gold
And twinkling expensive things,
But if all should come to be told
I meant to give a gift.

If I could post a poem
Delivered to the world
The subject: What we miss
And I would title it "Bliss."

God is a Multicolored Matrix

God is a multicolored matrix
Slinging colors all around,
In swirls and styles of many,
In shapes the most profound.

The eternal force in a measureless black,
Spotting here and there an externalization
Of good expression knowing not of evil,
In infinite love under illusory realness,

For God is a multicolored matrix
Seeking itself always in growth,
And the yearning of a bird in flight
Is the subliminal truth of infinite might.

God is many billions of people,
And planets, moons, stars,
Swirls and explosions of universal essence
Somewhere in our minds, out there in space,

Out there, in here, and all around,
I am It, It is You,
Truly, I am He
But always, all of That is You,

That is You and You are It,
Truly It is alive!
There is no divide
For God is a multicolored matrix.

www.ingramcontent.com/pod-product-compliance
Lightning Source LLC
Chambersburg PA
CBHW072048040426

42447CB00012BB/3072